FINDING

My Sunshine

AGAIN

FINDING
My Sunshine
AGAIN

AFTER **LOSS**, AND **SURVIVAL**

Deborah Ishida

gatekeeper press™

COLUMBUS, OHIO

FINDING MY SUNSHINE:
After Loss, and Survival

Published by Gatekeeper Press
2167 Stringtown Rd, Suite 109
Columbus, OH 43123-2989
www.GatekeeperPress.com

Library of Congress Control Number: 2021949479

ISBN (hardcover): 9781662921056
ISBN (paperback): 9781662921063
eISBN: 9781662921070

DEDICATION

*This book is dedicated to my
children Rebecca and Keith,
who knew and loved their father.
And to my grandchildren
Ethan and Emily
who never got to meet him,
but would have adored him.*

CONTENTS

INTRODUCTION

My book is for anyone who has loved and lost a spouse, or significant other. My husband was my sunshine, he warmed and nourished me, and I basked in the glow of our relationship.

His death at a very young age was devastating, and my years after his death have not always been easy.

I feel comforted in my belief, that wherever he is, he is happy. Once, when my son asked his father, "Dad, what is the meaning of life?", his father replied "Happiness, happiness is the meaning of life."

I often wondered if I would ever be happy again after his untimely death.

I have learned to find my sunshine again in the faces of my children, and grandchildren, and in the activities I have pursued.

I hope that when you read my book you can find that ray of hope that pierces the darkness, enabling you to find happiness again.

MY LIFE AS A CHILD

I was born on a rainy day in February 1942. My mother and my two older sisters—Ruth, six years old, and Jessica, one and a half—had been evacuated to the British countryside when the Germans severely bombed London. Of course we were not the only ones; millions of Londoners left their homes because of the devastation. Two million houses were damaged during the Blitz, 80% of these in London. Forty thousand civilians were killed, and many more injured. 1.5 million children, pregnant women, and other vulnerable people, such as the disabled, were sent to the countryside to avoid the bombs falling on London. My mother's sister Aunty Rae, her husband Alf, and their children Brenda and Irvin were evacuated to the same place, Bedfordshire. My mother rented a condemned cottage; why it was condemned, I never knew, but apparently my very industrious mother managed to make it a welcoming home.

My uncle Alf was the bus driver in our village, so when my mother went into labor with me, he drove her to the hospital. Poor people did not own their own cars. I was so tiny when I was born, full term but only about five pounds in weight, that a nurse put me in a vase as a joke, and I disappeared. My mother wasn't too impressed with this prank. When a tray was dropped on the floor I cried, and that told my mother that her third daughter could hear. My two older sisters had been born deaf, and since there was no deafness in the family, it was a puzzle. My father's sister had not been very kind about it and accused my mother Fanny of "giving Jack two deaf children."

We stayed in Bedfordshire until our little cottage burnt to the ground in a fire that was thought to be arson, but the perpetrators were never apprehended. So there was my mother with three little kids, and only the clothes on their backs. That mother of mine was a tough cookie; she epitomized the phrase "if the world gives you lemons, make lemonade."

Coming back to England, we lived in a London County Council (LCC) flat. The LCC is somewhat equivalent to subsidized housing for poor people. My father was a brilliant man, but coming from an impoverished family of seven kids, he could not pursue higher education. There were also a limited number of professions that

Jewish people could pursue at that time, and he had become a tailor. Not just any tailor, but a "bespoke" tailor, hand-making suits for men. The only trouble, besides not wanting to be a tailor, was that he was color-blind, and my mother had to often prevent him from sewing brown buttons on black suits and vice versa.

He loved to sing, had a lovely operatic voice, and would go around the house singing Caruso songs, especially on days when he would go to the track to bet on greyhound races. We had very little money, so my mother always argued with him: "Jack, where are you going? You know we don't have any money left over this week." He would respond, "I'm only taking a few shillings, and I'll win and bring home a lot of money." Well, he didn't win very often, and my mother would lock him out, only to have my sister Ruth creep to the door to let him in. I do remember him taking us to the Tower of London, and to other local places.

My mother was also very intelligent, but like my father had eight siblings, and could not go to high school. She went into dressmaking, and her boss would have her go to the local dress stores, look at the mannequins in the window, then come back and recreate the fashionable styles. She was very talented, and when she married my father she made her own wedding dress and all of the bridesmaid dresses. She was "lucky" to be married at 21 because in those times, at 21 you were considered to be "on the shelf."

My mother was one of six girls and three boys, and she was the oldest, therefore a lot of responsibilities fell on her shoulders. She used to tell me that she would put the kids to bed in one large bed, fitting them in like sardines.

My mother's mother, "Booba" (a name that all the grandmothers in my family are called), was a great cook. She had a kitchen the size of a postage stamp, but from there what dishes emerged—chicken, chicken soup with matzo balls, stuffed cabbage, kishka, etc. Even if you had eaten before visiting her, you had to eat again. She had a lady help her take care of things, and her name was Louie Deighton. My booba had gone to the "foundlings home" and picked her out to come home with her. Louie stayed for the rest of her life with my booba and zaida, and she called them Missus and Governor. She had big feet so she wore my grandfather's shoes. If you visited on the weekend, she would put her hand out and ask for "my wages." I remember her complaining that she had to eat a lot of chicken feet, but she was an integral part of the family.

My maternal grandfather was a shoe repairer, and I can see him now, holding nails in his mouth and spitting them out one at a time to hammer into the sole of a shoe. They lived in the West End of London, and we lived in the East End. Some of the other siblings lived in Highgate, in northern London. We had large family get-togethers in Highgate for every major Jewish holiday. I remember platters upon platters of food coming out of the kitchen, and in the midst of it all large numbers of cats spilling out of the basement.

My father's sister, Aunty Leah, loved the way my mother cooked fish, and fish was cheap in those days. My mother would get a large cod and have the fish shop cut it into rounds, dip the slices in egg and matzo meal and fry them up golden brown. Aunty Leah would come for dinner, and then take a large portion of the fish home with her. My mother would pull me aside and tell me to say that we had already eaten, and we were going to have a cheese sandwich in the kitchen. I told her, "No, I want fish, not a cheese sandwich," but I never won.

My father had other siblings, including Milly, Barney, Ray and

Ellen, and he had a brother Keith who was killed in the war at age 19.

Where we lived there was a large playground on the street level, and all the kids played there. For the most part we all got along really well. My mother would make toffee apples on sticks, and the kids would gobble them up. At suppertime calls would go out: "Mrs. Rapaport has fish and chips, I'm eating at her house." There were times, however, when some kids taunted my sisters, making faces and calling out "deaf and dumb, deaf and dumb." I would come to their defense and swing my little fists at them to drive them away.

After we had returned to London, my mother had her last child, Keith, named after my father's brother who had died in the war. Keith had full hearing, and was four years younger than me.

As I mentioned, we were poor, but we all looked out for each other in the building. One day my mother cut our small chicken in half and told me to take one half next door to the Schwartzes, because her husband had lost his job. She was so thankful, and told me to tell my mother that it was a mitzvah (a good deed). I looked at the puny half a chicken left behind, and wondered how it could possibly feed six people. But with her unflappable nature, my mother made sauerkraut, lots of potatoes, and bits of chicken for everyone, saving the largest piece for my father.

When we were lucky we had Smarties for a treat; they are like M&Ms but came in a tube. One day my mother laid out four equal rows for the four kids, and told us to collect our Smarties. Now, I was a very methodical child; I thought about everything before I did it, and was meticulous. My mother said I even folded my own dirty underwear. I was eating my Smarties one at a time, with a long break in between each one, when my sister Jessica sidled up to me and asked me for two of my Smarties. I refused, explaining to her that these were mine, and if she had eaten hers, well, she had her share. She asked me again for two Smarties, again I refused, so she got some scissors and cut off two of my lovely long curls. I screamed out loud, and my mother came running in and also started screaming. Before my father came home, she quickly rearranged my hair into a different hairstyle to cover up the missing curls. In came my father, took one look at me and said, "Fanny, what did you do to Deborah's hair?" to which she replied, "Oh, I tried a different style." He said, "I like the old one better." I always say, "Thank God Jessica didn't ask for five Smarties—I would have been bald."

My mother believed in the value of a good education, and I was a smart girl. I went to Spital Square high school, which was in the middle of a fruit and vegetable market. We had uniforms, but my mother couldn't afford them, so she made my uniform. The material wasn't exactly the same, the checks were bigger, and some of the popular (mean) girls giggled and pointed at me. "Her mother made her uniform, she's poor, hee hee."

Those same girls would sit together at recess styling each other's hair, or trying out makeup, and of course I was not invited. I had a very good friend, Sheila Bryant, who was in the same grade as myself, but who was much taller than me. We were paired up as dancemates, and we enjoyed a great friendship that has endured till this day. We were called "the tall and the short of it."

One day before school I was sitting with my mum in the kitchen, near the radiator, because it was cold in the house, and I was having a cup of tea. I began to feel poorly, then fell off my stool and hit my head on the radiator. I woke up to find my mum standing over me.

She slapped me for scaring her, then sent me to school. Now, my mum wasn't mean or an abuser, but she lived vicariously through me, and couldn't stand the thought of me missing a day of school.

She loved my sisters Ruth and Jessica very much, and wanted them to have the very best possible education, and the best education was in the Jewish deaf school in Clapham, a residential school a train ride away from us. They went there, and we saw them as often as we could, and always at vacation time. They often brought home other children with them who lived in far-off countries, and could not go home for the vacations.

As I got older, my mother would tell me that if I didn't want to help take care of them, I was selfish, because I was hearing. This reminder of my responsibility as a hearing person has really caused me to be a perpetual caregiver.

We would go on inexpensive bus trips as a family, and one of the places I remember was Southend, where there was a nice beach. I recall an occasion when my mother brought lunch, and one thing was a whole cooked chicken. It was very windy that day, and the sand blew into the chicken. I doubt that my mother would have thrown it away; I bet she gave it a salt water bath in the ocean!

We were friends with a family in our building, parents Sol and Lilly Graff, and kids Pauline and Alan. To save money, Lilly would often go to a store that sold cans without their labels (I guess they had slipped off in transport, so that every can was a mystery waiting to be discovered). I know she used to shake the can to hear if it might contain peaches, but 99% of the time she came away with beets. Sol would say as he opened his sandwich, "Oh no, beets and onions again."

I began dating Alan when I was 15 and he was a couple of years older, and had a barrow in the market where he sold fabric. Lilly felt we should get married early, and that Alan would be able to support me very well from his business. My mother, on the other hand, did not want this for me, and told Lily that I was smart and that she thought I should go to college. I think she thought that was an insult to her, Alan and her family, but my mother was right. Although Alan was a special person, we did not last when I went away to university.

I was 17 when I graduated high school, and I was equally gifted in the arts and sciences. I loved to act, but I knew deep down that it was highly unlikely that I could make a living at that, and I needed to support myself. I could have done a combination of science and medical school that would have taken five years, but I didn't. The reason for that is that one of the teachers relayed a story to me of going for a medical school interview and seeing six people dissect a human arm. That story dismayed me for years.

I could have gone to Cambridge University, but they wanted me to wait till I was 18, and I was impatient to start my university training. I went to Southampton University on a scholarship that covered room and board, books and tuition. However, I only had ten shillings a month left over, and that was a pittance. My mother said that they could buy me a pair of stockings once in a while, and they did.

At Southampton University I studied physiology, biochemistry, chemistry and math, and lived in the women's dorm. At dinner we had to wear our black robes, and food was served at large tables on platters. To be very honest, the platters were better than the food. You would lift off the top of the tureen to discover runny mashed potatoes underneath. I liked to serve because I was fast, and liked to eat my food when it was hot. One of my table mates, Mary Ann, was a skinny little thing, with a mop of golden curls and a voracious appetite. No matter what they were serving, she always had seconds, but I don't know where she put them.

I had many friends at university—Margaret, Pat, Sally, and many more. I met Alan Lindsay when we went to the popular dance they had every Friday, and we became an item. We loved each other, but his parents objected to us being a couple because I was Jewish, and they were antisemitic, so that ended.

I did very well at university, but couldn't go home frequently because we couldn't spare the train fare. Many of the other students would go home in their chauffeur driven cars, and after asking me several times when my car was coming for me, they stopped asking. My father would always meet me at the local train station, and we would walk home together, sharing things that had occurred in my absence. One time he picked up my little suitcase and then put it down, obviously short of breath. This was so unlike him; he was short and wiry, but usually very strong. He said, "Deborah, you need to have a rest." I didn't, but obviously he did, and I was worried. At home I noticed that my father would become very moody, screaming for no reason, and displaying a very short temper. This was not my dad.

Shortly after my return to university, I received a phone call from my mom telling me that my father was having seizures. She had taken him to the doctor, where they learned he had a brain tumor. There were debates about whether to have surgery performed, but the doctor informed my mother and father that the tumor was a glioblastoma multiforme, and that they would not be able to remove it, because that kind of cancer had tentacles like an octopus that invaded deep into the brain.

My father decided that he would not have a useless surgery, and would live out his life at home. When one of his sisters heard this, she was incensed, and accused my mother of not wanting him to have surgery because she wanted him to die. That was so very cruel and untrue. My mother just didn't want him to go through a useless procedure. She loved my father.

My father listened to his sister and had surgery, which of course was not curative, and made him weaker. I went to see him one day in the hospital, asked for Jacob Rapaport, and was directed to a skeletal old man on a stretcher. I told them that they had made a mistake, that my father was young and strong, not skeletal. But that was my father lying there, and not long after he died. I think it was nine months from diagnosis to death.

I finished university with a very good degree, an Upper 2nd, and was preparing to do post grad work or get a job. Little did I know that my time in England was coming to a close. In 1958 my sister met a young man who had been born in Czechoslovakia (now the Czech Republic). He had survived the Holocaust and was now living in Sweden. He was travelling to England on a vacation from his job, and was going to the London chess championships. He was a very good chess player, but could not compete because he was "stateless," so he observed as a fan. He went to the Jewish deaf club in London and met my sister Jessica there, and there was a mutual attraction. He returned to Sweden and they corresponded by letters.

Harry eventually decided to move to Los Angeles, where some of his siblings resided, and he asked Jessica to come out with him. By then my father was very ill. She agreed to go. It was October 1960, and they got married on December 25th of that year. After a while they purchased a little house, and settled into a happy married life. My father died in January 1961, about a week after Jessica and Harry's honeymoon. I was in my final year at Southampton University, and when I graduated my mother decided that since my father had died, we would all go to the US to be with Jessica and her husband Harry. I wasn't sure that I wanted to go—my life was in England—but my brother Keith had already been sent to LA, my sister Ruth and her family had also decided to go, and I wasn't thrilled about staying by myself.

I crossed the pond with my mother in 1962 and went to stay for a little while with her sister Rosie and her husband Bill, in Far Rockaway, New York. My mum and I were strolling the boardwalk one day when she said, "Deborah, I know that lady coming towards us. Her name is Rachel and I went to school with her."

"Mom, don't be ridiculous," I replied. "She looks like a tiny speck from here. How can you know who she is?"

The tiny speck approached and got bigger. "I'm Fanny," my mum said to her. "Aren't you Rachel? We went to school together in west London."

"Oh yes, that's right!"

They chatted and then said their goodbyes. I don't think I ever doubted my mother's powers of observation again.

We went to stay with Jessica and Harry in Los Angeles, and they made us very welcome. Jessica thought that I should get a boyfriend, so she told me about this young man she had heard about who would like to date me. I wanted to know more about him, so I called him up and asked him to tell me about himself. Sam said, "I'm tall and ugly, with bad acne." I laughed because it was refreshing to hear a humorous story, so I agreed to go on a date. The evening arrived and there stood Sam…tall, ugly and with acne. He had been telling the truth. To be honest, I am not sure anymore if I did go on that date after all.

My mother, my brother Keith, and I rented an apartment on Robertson Boulevard. It was a one-bedroom, which my mother and I shared, while Keith slept on a pull-out sofa in the living room. When we first moved in, we slept on the floor until we could pay for furniture. My mother did not want to buy on credit; she said it wasn't how they did it in England.

I started to look for a job, partly because I wanted to work, and partly because financially I needed to contribute to our household expenses. I saw an advertisement in the Los Angeles Times for a laboratory assistant at the UCLA Neuropsychiatric Center. I applied, had an interview and was hired. Dr. Sydney Roberts said the work I showed him from Southampton University was the equivalent of PhD work in America.

My mother was working as a seamstress in Ohrbach's, a department store in mid-Wilshire. Keith was going to SMCC , and I was now employed. We were settling into our new life in this great new land.

My immediate boss at work was Dr. Claire Zomzely. She had a PhD, and was doing some of the original work on protein synthesis in rat brain ribosomes. In order to collect the ribosomes, we had to kill rats, take out their brains, and extract ribosomes from there. At first we weren't sure that ribosomes could be frozen, so we had long days getting the ribosomes and then immediately doing our experiments. We later found out that they could be frozen and still function, so we were able to freeze them. One day I tripped while coming out of the freezer with a whole tray of ribosomes in my hand, and smashed all the vials. A whole day's work down the drain. That was a sad day for us.

One day Claire announced that she was going to see Dr. Roberts to discuss the progress of our work. "Hold on, Claire," I replied. "I'm just about ready."

There was silence, and then she answered, "I'm sorry, but you're not invited."

"Not invited? Why not? I worked on the project with you."

Claire said, "You don't have the passport. You need an MD or a PhD to be considered an equal partner."

I was furious, and said, "It takes four years to get an MD," to which she calmly replied, "Where will you be in four years if you don't do it?" That set a fire under my behind, and I applied to many medical schools, getting into almost all of them. I interviewed at UCLA, my first choice, because I could live at home and not have to pay for room and board.

My interviewer was Dr. Thompson, a surgeon with a Scottish brogue who had a reputation for throwing scalpels at nurses in the operating room. He asked me what specialty I wanted to go into after I graduated from medical school, and I said surgery. "Surgery?" he said with surprise. "You're a woman. Don't you want to get married and have children?" I replied, "Can't I do both?"

I got into UCLA, graduating class of 1969, with 70 men and 3 women. The men were not too happy to have us as classmates, because they saw us as taking away a place from a more deserving male!

I purchased a car, then my brother Keith asked if he could use it so he could get to SMCC faster than riding the bus. I agreed because I could take the bus to UCLA. After a while I got fed up with taking the bus, and asked for my car back, so Keith purchased a scooter. He had a part time job at Ohrbach's, and one day before going to work he gave his nieces and nephews rides around the block. Waving goodbye, he left for work, and was hit at the intersection while making a left turn. Despite wearing a helmet, he was left decerebrate, and I saw him at USC on life support with tubes coming out of every orifice. He died, and I could not bear to see him in his coffin. I was devastated, felt very guilty, and to this day I have not forgiven myself for his death. I have been to counselling, cried over his grave, and listened to people who said it was my car and I had a right to take it back. Others say it was his time, and if it hadn't been that I took my car back, he would have died young in some other way. He was only 19 years old, and I had killed him.

I wanted to quit medical school, but my mother wouldn't let me entertain that idea. So back to medical school I went, and it was horrific because in anatomy class we were dissecting a human cadaver.

Slowly, very slowly, I began to focus on medical school again, and I also met a fellow classmate named Jim Scully. Jim was a tall red-haired guy of Irish American background, and he was a Catholic. We started to date, and became romantic partners. I thought I would eventually marry him. We would go to San Blas in Mexico whenever we could over a long weekend, and he even got me an opal engagement ring.

He introduced me to his family. He was one of seven siblings; his mother had converted to Catholicism, and was a fervent Catholic. When she didn't want any more children, she banished Jim's father and a mentally challenged sibling to the garage. When the father asked me my surname, and I said it was Rapaport, he asked me where it was from. I told him it was Polish Jewish, and he wasn't pleased that his son was dating a Jew. Later on he warmed up to me, and even bought some Jewish records, to show I was okay.

Jim kept a large python in a cage in the bathroom, and I tried not to have to go to the toilet during my visits to his house. That python terrified me.

One year Jim went to Mexico with another classmate who was having some difficulties at school, and came back with a Mexican girlfriend! I guess that meant that we were no longer a couple! Later on he would marry Rae, an African American nurse he met on one of his rotations.

I MEET KIBI

In September 1968 I went to a dance at the International Students Center on Hilgard Avenue, to get away from medical school, and met Kibimaro Ishida at the door. He was a year behind me in medical school, and was Japanese American. He too had wanted a break from the grind. I can still hear his voice: "Wanna dance?"

Who is this short nerdy Japanese-American guy with a crappy haircut, large Adam's apple, plastic pocket protector and polyester clothes? He's not my type at all! But I agreed to dance with him because I felt sorry for him. Later he told me, "Deb, I asked you to dance because I didn't think anyone would dance with someone wearing such an ugly dress." Remember how I told you my mother was a seamstress, but we were poor? Well, she had made my dress out of a piece of fabric she could afford, and it was lizard green, not the most flattering of colors.

He never left my side all night, and after the dance he invited me back to his dorm, made me fresh brewed coffee, and offered me some carrot cake he had made. He was beginning to look better and better! I was used to tea, and if I had coffee it was the instant kind, so having freshly brewed coffee was a treat. And he could also bake!

We started to date, and my mother fell in love with him. "Deborah, this one's a keeper," she said to me more than once. He kept her company when I was on duty at the hospital, further endearing himself to her, which she would tell me all about: "Deborah, Kibi came over. It was so nice of him. He's so sweet, and he always wears that dark blue beanie when he washes his hair. I think it suits him."

At Christmas time he asked me to visit his family in San Francisco. He was one of seven children, four boys and three girls, and he was the second youngest. There were only six children still alive; his oldest brother Hidemaro had presumably been killed during the Korean War in 1951. He had volunteered to fight there because he wanted to show his loyalty to America. Don't forget that Roosevelt had ordered 120,000 people of Japanese descent into the internment camps in February 1942, and two-thirds of them were American citizens. Kibi was born in the Crystal City Internment Camp in 1944, and his youngest brother Kazumaro was also born there in 1946. The loyalty of Japanese-Americans was often questioned in those years, and Hidemaro wanted to show he was a patriotic American.

He had poor vision, but you were not able to wear glasses in the position he was applying for, so he memorized the eye chart and got in as a right tail gunner on a B-29. His plane was shot down on his 21st mission, which was his next-to-last or last mission. I say 'presumably' killed because he was apparently captured when his plane went down, and he was never heard from again. His family was left to grieve his loss at the tender age of 19. How awful it must have been for his parents to lose their oldest son, and for his siblings to lose their brother.

During our Christmas visit one of Kibi's sisters, Renko, asked, "Are you two planning on getting married anytime soon? Because we're all here!" We had only been together for four months, but we looked at each other and said yes! Kibi was such a loving, caring human being. I didn't need years to know his worth.

Coming from a large family, Kibi had wanted to help out with expenses, so he worked for a shipping magazine that sent out details about the movement of ships and their schedules.

His parents mainly spoke Japanese, so his oldest sister Taeko helped by going to the PTA meetings, and to other places where a parental figure was needed. She was fifteen years older than Kibi, and he really looked up to her.

His father, Archbishop Nitten Ishida, as well as being a Buddhist priest was a calligraphy artist. He taught calligraphy to students at the church, made wonderful scrolls, and even designed artwork for Akira Kurosawa's famous movie Ran. Kibi's mother Chiyoko Ishida taught tea ceremony and ikebana (Japanese flower arranging). She was also honored as "mother of the year" several times in San Francisco.

All of the children had at least a Master's degree, and some higher than that. My amazing Kibi did a double major in physics and mathematics at the University of California Berkeley. I was so lucky to be marrying into a wonderful family.

KIBI AND I MARRY

We bought plain gold bands, because that's all we could afford; and what do you know, Renko's wedding dress was hanging in the closet. She was tiny, but it fit me to a T, so I wore it. Thank goodness I was petite at the time, because that dress would not fit me now. Because it was such short notice, my mother was the only one from my side of the family who could attend. The pillbox hat that completed the wedding outfit needed to be secured more firmly on my head, so my mother made two loops through which you could put hairpins, and thus make it stable. She made the loops too large, and to this day whenever I look at my wedding pictures I laugh, because those loops are so prominent. It's strange, isn't it, that you can vividly remember small things like that from years ago, and sometimes don't remember what you ate for breakfast!

Kibi's father was an archbishop in the Nichiren Buddhist Church, and they had a sanctuary in their church basement on Pine Street.

We were married there by his father, and I said my vows in Japanese. To this day I do not know what I promised my dear husband. This Jewish girl became the Jewish girl with the Japanese name. Oh, what a feast we had in the church basement! It was January 1st, so it was also the Japanese new year. Family and friends packed the tables. We ate and drank and it was wonderful.

I was now a married woman. Kibi, myself and my mother drove back to Los Angeles in his VW bug. We went to live with my mother, and we both returned to medical school. We then decided to get a place of our own, and moved into a one-bedroom apartment in nearby Venice, California.

WE START
A FAMILY

Three months after we got married, I was pregnant. The apartment we lived in did not allow children, so we moved back in with my mother. She was as happy as a clam, because as I have said, she loved Kibi. In fact, she pulled me aside one day and said with a smile, "I don't know how to tell you, but I love Kibi more than I love you."

I said, "Don't feel bad, Mom. I've known that since the day you met him."

The OB-GYN doctor told us that I had a contracted pelvis, but since we were small people, my baby would most likely be under seven and a half pounds, and therefore I should have no difficulty delivering the baby. I went into labor, the progress stopped, an X-ray was taken of my pelvis, and it was determined that I couldn't have even a four-pound child vaginally.

Rebecca Kimiko Ishida was born on January 29th 1970 by Caesarean section, and she was beautiful. Unfortunately her hospital baby pictures were lost, so she often asked if she was adopted. I wish those baby pictures had not been lost. I bottle-fed her because I had to return to work. My mother took care of her for me, and she loved to do it.

Three months after Rebecca was born, I was pregnant again with Keith, and people 'joked,' "Don't you guys do anything else? Don't you watch TV?" Keith Hidemaro Ishida was born February 12th, 1971, and I breast-fed Keith till he bit me, causing mastitis (an infection in the breast), at which point I switched him to a cup.

Shortly after Keith's birth, Kibi came home walking awkwardly. "Kibi," I said, "you're walking like a duck. What's the problem?" He said he had had a vasectomy. I was floored. True, I didn't like diaphragms and couldn't tolerate birth control pills, and he disliked condoms, but he could have discussed it with me first before making a unilateral decision. I probably wanted more children. Dear Kibi didn't want us to overpopulate the world!

When I went back to work, my mother watched both kids, and for her it was a labor of love. I had graduated from UCLA medical school in 1969, and Kibi in 1970, and we were both working at post-grad programs.

We were busy but happy, and Kibi was an equal partner in helping with the kids. If he came home first he would make dinner, and if I came home first I did. He also changed diapers without making a fuss. I thought this was normal, and that was the way all couples cooperated, but of course that is not true. Kibi was a treasure, a true equal partner, we loved each other. How very lucky we were.

WE GO TO GERMANY

The Vietnam War was waging, and doctors were being drafted. The only way to be able to complete your training before being drafted was to apply for the Berry Plan. This allowed you to defer your service till you had completed your residency. Kibi was accepted, and then he had to decide where to serve. We both wanted Tripler Hospital in Hawaii, but Kibi pointed out that it was going to be difficult to get it, because it was so popular. Most of the European bases were in Germany, and because we had decided that we preferred to leave America and go on an adventure, Kibi asked me this question: "Deb, how would you feel if we went to Germany? You lost a lot of relatives in the Holocaust; could you tolerate being stationed in Germany for three years?" I thought about it and said that as long as he was by my side I could tolerate anything. He was my knight in shining armor.

The Vietnam War ended, but because he had committed to the Berry Plan, in 1973 off we went to Germany—Kibi, myself, our children Rebecca and Keith, and my mom. Our destination was the Army's 33rd Field Hospital in Wurzburg. There was no on-base housing available, so we rented in a small village called Rottenbauer, not too far from the hospital. Our landlord worked in a beer factory, so every night we were greeted with, "Prost, here's a beer for you." Life was good, and Germany was beautiful.

When Kibi first reported to work, his boss Colonel Omer, a very large and imposing figure, asked Kibi if it was true that his wife was a doctor. Kibi said yes, and Omer told him he needed a doctor in the outpatient clinic, and to ask me if I wanted to work. I decided to accept the position as a GS-13, a high-ranking civilian position.

My mother watched the kids, then when they were old enough they went to kindergarten. Kibi and I worked hard, and he even ran a hepatitis ward, fueled by the drug use of the new volunteer army. Our son Keith did not like being in school and tried to run away, but he was brought back into the classroom. There was no disobeying his strict teachers.

We had fun during our three years in Germany, going on volksmarches in the German countryside, and going on vacation as a family. We went to the Black Forest, Luxembourg, Majorca, Switzerland, and many many more places, including every petting zoo!

I can still visualize Kibi holding one or another of the kids on his shoulders and smiling as we walked through the German countryside. He was a great dad who loved his children, and they loved him back. However, although we loved Germany, we were upset when the kids were taunted by German kids with cries of "Ching Chong" because of their ethnicity. We had to have a talk with them about intermarriage, racism, and people who do not accept you for who you are.

Kibi and I also had some "alone time" when we visited Holland, Norway, Denmark and Sweden, while Mom took care of Keith and Rebecca. I always loved our time together. Kibi was a loving, fun, supportive husband.

During our stay in Germany, we got a phone call in the middle of the night from my sister Jessica, who lived in Beverly Hills. "Deborah," she said, "there's a house for sale here in Beverly Hills for $75,000. You should grab it." My response was that it was the middle of the night, and the price was too high! How I would eat my words when we eventually looked for and bought a much pricier house upon our return to Los Angeles.

When we came back to Beverly Hills, we rented an apartment on Elm Street near Beverly Vista School, and the kids both went to school there. Kibi went to work as an internist at the local Kaiser Permanente medical center on Cadillac Avenue, just a few miles from our apartment, and I went to work at the same hospital as a family practice M.D. I had been accepted into a dermatology residency at UCLA, so I was supposed to only remain at Kaiser for a few months.

As the date approached for the start of the residency, I began to get anxious (and I am not sure why). I began to ask people what dermatologists typically treat, and they said "mostly warts and acne." This turned me off, so one day without really thinking it through, I called up and withdrew from the residency. Oh, what a stupid mistake I made! Dermatology is not just warts and acne, and I would have loved it. Instead I stayed at Kaiser for many years. I was a good M.D., but dermatology would have been a great fit for me. Now when I see that reality show "Dr. Pimple Popper" on TV, I say to myself, I could have been Dr. Pimple Popper. I don't say that out of regret for the fame and money, but out of regret for my foolish career decision.

Life was good, busy but enjoyable. Kibi and I worked, the kids went to school, and my mother cooked, kept house and babysat. Mom was a very good cook, and I found her meatballs especially delicious. One day they didn't taste the same, and when I asked her about that she told me that she had put soy sauce in them "for Kibi." I told her that I knew she loved him, but could I please have my old meatballs back?

After living in the apartment for a while, we decided to look for a house, and found the one where I still live. We put down $40,000 that we had saved up from being in the Army, and took on a $100,000 mortgage. As I said before, the house that my sister had suggested for $75,000 had been a bargain.

FAMILY
VACATIONS

At the clinic where we both worked, Kibi and I would put in for vacation at the same time, and we would have time off each January and July. We went on so many trips as a family, very frequently to six of the seven Hawaiian islands. What adventures we had swimming, snorkeling, attending luaus, going on boat trips, and doing lots of hula dances. We also went to Greece, Israel, Jamaica, Fiji, Australia and New Zealand, as well as to many states in the US. One highlight was the M Bar J horse ranch, where there was a pond stocked with bluegill and wonderful horses to ride.

Other doctors were buying houses and boats, but we preferred the thrill of seeing new places and spending time with each other. Our house was busy with lots of kids coming over, mainly because when we remodeled to put on a second story, we added a pool.

Kibi taught Keith to fish, and the two of them would sometimes go out on a fishing boat or to a lake or pier, and they brought home lots of fish. Kibi was a very good cook as well, and both of them were great fish filleters, so we regularly had fabulous fish dinners. Kibi's masterpiece was an Asian whole steamed fish drizzled with peanut oil, a touch of sesame oil, grated ginger and soy sauce. My mouth remembers it even now.

Kibi and I were a very good team. We worked well together at home, and loved each other deeply. And how the years flew by! The kids finished elementary school, middle school and high school. Rebecca went on to the University of California Santa Barbara, and finished in four years. She lived in the dormitories, then in a house with other students, and had especially liked her human sexuality classes. She was a teacher's assistant in human sexuality, and was very successful at it.

Keith wasn't crazy about higher education, which was very hard on him. He did go to Santa Monica Community College, but never got his AA. He ended up going to Israel to work on a kibbutz, and also designed and manufactured a "head tail hat" which he patented.

The stories from the kibbutz were great, and since he liked fish he had been assigned to the fish ponds where tilapia were raised. He had to get up very early to take care of them "at the crack of dawn," so he quit that job. He then was assigned to the kitchen, but hated that because "the dishwasher was the size of a carwash." He ended up parting ways with the kibbutz.

In 1994 Kibi, myself and the two kids went to Australia and New Zealand, with a layover in Fiji. What a marvelous adventure it was. We saw the north and south islands of New Zealand, both so very different. In the north there were fjords, and in the south geysers. We feasted on corn on the cob that had been cooked in the boiling water coming from the geysers. We also visited glow worm caves, and had many other fantastic memories. If you've never been to a glow worm cave, please go. You enter into the darkness, and suddenly the walls of the cave are illuminated with thousands of points of light, a truly spectacular sight

We snorkeled the Great Barrier Reef, saw the Sydney Opera House, went to the beautiful beaches, and ate great food. One of the highlights was when all four of us climbed to the top of Ayers Rock, a difficult but amazing climb. It really was the trip of a lifetime. The natives call the rock Uluru, and it is sacred to them, and they do not really want tourists climbing it. Maybe we shouldn't have done it, but our only excuse was that we were not the only ones.

KIBI GETS BACK PAIN
A DIAGNOSIS
AND TREATMENT

Because we went to so many places, slept in many different hotels, dragged luggage around, and travelled by plane, trains and buses, it didn't seem so unusual that Kibi had some back pain when he came home. He attributed it to "just a pulled muscle." At first I accepted it, but he began to have pain that woke him up at night, and that was "a red flag," because muscle pain gets better from lying down, not worse.

One night I noticed him at the side of the bed holding his right flank, and again he said "it's nothing." I wasn't buying that, because he should have been more comfortable lying down. I persuaded him to see a Physical Medicine doctor, and they ordered an MRI of his back, to rule out a slipped disc. We were elated when it came back negative, but it turned out to be a false negative; they had missed a tumor stripe in front of the spine, and of course we didn't know that.

I was at my desk in the Klotz Student Health Center, part of California State University at Northridge, where I now worked because I had wanted to start seeing more teenagers, when I got a call from Kibi. That was unusual; although we loved each other, we never disturbed each other at work with routine stuff, but rather talked about those things at night when we got home.

Kibi said, "Deborah, I was short of breath climbing the stairs at work, so my friend persuaded me to get a chest X-ray. It turns out I have fluid in my lungs, and I'm getting it tapped today." My heart sank to my boots, the room spun, my heart pounded, and I almost fainted, but I managed to ask him who was going to do the procedure, and he said Dr. Suh. I immediately called him up and asked him to please let me know the results of the fluid he removed.

Soon after I got a call. "Deborah, I'm sorry, but Kibi has Non-Hodgkin's Lymphoma."

"No, no, no!" I screamed. "It can't be! It can't be!" I dissolved into a puddle of tears at my desk. I had a very bad premonition that our life as we knew it was irrevocably changed. My Kibi, my love, couldn't have NHL. I wouldn't allow it! I left work and came home across the 405 freeway, sobbing all the way. I still don't know how I made that trip back to the house.

I barged in through the door to find my dear husband sitting in a chair in front of the TV, eating a pizza. "Deborah," he said, "I have NHL and I'm eating this pizza." Then he added, "I'm a good guy. Why couldn't I have just broken my ankle?"

TThis must be a mistake, a bad dream, a nightmare, I thought. He can't have NHL, he can't be sick. He's a strong healthy man. It was only months ago that we climbed Uluru.

We made an appointment to see the oncologist, and his first words to us were, "You're lucky, Kibi. You have Diffuse Large B-Cell NHL, and it has a 70 percent cure rate." Then he threw in, "It's the same type of lymphoma that Jackie Kennedy Onassis had." I pointed out to him that somehow I didn't feel so lucky, because she had died of the illness. I had a dreadful feeling that our life was not going to be the wondrous adventure we had thought it would be.

He advised us that Kibi should start chemotherapy right away, for a tumor the CAT scan had revealed was the size of a pack of cards. It was retroperitoneal, behind the peritoneum (the serous membrane lining the cavity of the abdomen and covering the abdominal organs). He had back pain at night, because when he lay down the tumor pressed on the nerves. Maybe if Kibi was a complainer, he would have spoken out earlier about his back pain, but he was stoic. If we had caught it earlier, the tumor would have been smaller.

Kibi started chemotherapy, and it was awful—nausea, vomiting, no appetite and extreme exhaustion. He also lost his lovely thick black hair that fell in chunks onto the pillow. It was so hard to see that happening, I shaved his head. He asked for a tape recorder, and while not a comedic fellow at all, he recorded, "Thank you, chemotherapy, for this marvelous haircut."

His chemotherapy was every 21 days, and for at least 11 of them he was completely wiped out. We loved Cajun Zydeco dancing, so if Kibi felt a tiny bit better we would go to a dance. All the single ladies loved him, so with his indwelling port through which he could receive his chemotherapy, African hat on his head, and their head on his shoulder, they danced to the music. So many of them wanted to dance with him that I had to say, "Kibi, save a slow dance for your wife!"

We also joined a support group, patients in one group and loved ones in another, and we all bonded and poured our hearts out to one another. The vast majority of people were heartbroken about their loved ones' illnesses, and some patients even died while we were in the group. One lady was more angry than sad because her husband had lied to her; he was a smoker, and she had told him that she would leave him if he didn't quit, so he reassured her that he had. She later found out that he had been lying to her, had kept on smoking, and had covered the smell of tobacco breath up with mints, sprays and mouthwashes. When he died of lung cancer, she was so angry with him for deceiving her.

During one session, a lady spoke up who had cared for her boyfriend during his back-to-back stem cell transplants. He had been separated from his wife, and this lady had been his devoted lover and caregiver. She had been told that if he died, she would be allowed to remain in their condo afterwards. Well, he had obviously not put those instructions into his will, because immediately after his death his son threw her out, and all she got were "Steve's ashes in a box," as she put it. What thanks for having taken care of him over his painful, prolonged illness.

One other lady in the group who had a husband named Jack joined in. "Oh, you got Steve in a box. I wonder what it would be like to have Jack in a box?" We all screamed with merriment. We had found laughter in the midst of sorrow, when we believed that we would never be able to laugh ever again.

No matter how sick Kibi was, he always managed to go and visit my mother in her apartment, take her for a walk around the block, and fill up her weekly medications. He was a very kind person, and had been so since he was a boy. His younger brother Kazumaro remembers an occasion as children when he had told Kibi that he wished he could be more like him, a math and chemistry whiz who was very skillful at building things with his hands. Kibi had turned to him and said, "Kaz, you are a kind and warm-hearted person. You are a fantastic person. I wish I could be more like you."

Wow, I had truly lucked out when I married Kibi.

WE GET
BLINDSIDED

Kibi completed his chemotherapy, and was told he was in remission. Oh happy day! We laughed and cried at the same time, and felt so fortunate.

"I love you, Kibi," I said.

"I love you, Deborah," he replied. "How lucky we are. We're going to grow old together. We beat this thing."

Our wedding anniversary was January 1st, so at the end of December Kibi and I went to Hawaii to celebrate. We had so much fun. We went to a New Year's party at a little club that said "$5 entrance, no refunds," and ate and travelled. One thing I remember vividly was going to an "all you can eat" buffet and seeing three very large Polynesian gentlemen belly up to the buffet. They heaped up plate after plate, just swallowing them down, and Kibi and I told each other that the restaurant would have to close because it was going to run out of food. It was so good to be laughing again after such a grueling time. We were young and in love, Kibi was in remission, and all was right with the world.

Then everything went dark again. Kibi was sitting in the hotel room and said, "Deb, I don't know why, but my back is hurting." I asked him where, and he pointed to his right flank, the same area in which he had first had his pain. I knew in my heart of hearts that this was terrible news, so when we got back to LA I told him he needed to see his oncologist. She ordered a plain X-ray of his abdomen, and told him it was negative. I know I could have said that we need a CAT scan, but I was in a very frightened state, and felt that we needed something done now.

I told Kibi that we needed a second opinion. My husband was very reluctant to go, but I persuaded him, and we saw an oncologist at

USC. After listening to the history, he agreed that, because the pain was in the original place that the cancer had been, we needed a CAT scan. This was done at Kibi's hospital, and it showed that either the cancer had never gone away, or had recurred. What a devastating blow. We had been told he was in remission, and now we were kicked in the gut. We cried, we hugged, we wondered about the future, and we prayed.

We saw the oncologist again and she told us that the only hope was a stem cell transplant. Stem cells are the original cells you generate, often called the body's "raw materials," that then eventually differentiate into all of your blood cells and tissue cells. A stem cell transplant is a very tough treatment in which your own stem cells are harvested from your blood, you are given very powerful chemotherapy to wipe out all of your cancer cells, and then the stem cells are infused back, hopefully to repopulate your bone marrow with new cancer-free cells.

A major drawback is that the chemotherapy wipes out good cells as well as bad, leaving you in a very vulnerable position for getting an infection, or even dying if the stem cells don't "take." We had no choice, though, so Kibi agreed to the procedure. We both desperately wanted him to live. He was my rock, I was his love, and he had to survive.

I don't know if you can imagine the emotion of seeing your beloved husband, a perfectly healthy man till very recently, sitting in a chair in a hospital, with tubes coming out of him to remove his blood, searching for the life-saving stem cells. This procedure had to be repeated many times until enough stem cells were harvested. Here we were, both of us doctors, and both unable to make inroads into this lymphoma that was usurping my husband's body.

I tried to keep a positive vibe going for him, but I found it almost impossible. I felt like an actor wearing a two-sided theater mask; on one side I was trying to be positive, but my real feelings of sadness were on the other side of the mask. I was terrified for the future. Would he make it?

THE STEM CELL
IMPLANT

Finally the stem cells had been harvested and stored, and it was time for Kibi to enter the hospital for this life-saving procedure. He was treated with very powerful chemotherapy agents that wiped out his bone marrow, and he was very very weak. Because of the increased risk of infection, we had to wear gowns and masks.

I would go into his hospital room and hear the tape of "Somewhere Over the Rainbow" sung by Hawaiian artist Israel Kamakawiwo'ole, and see my beloved husband sleeping or tapping his fingers on the sheet to the music. Memories flooded my mind—the multiple trips to Hawaii with the family, the smell of flowers, the hula shows, the beautiful warm waters, how happy we were. For a while I was there in those happier times, then I was pulled back into reality. This song was not being sung in that wondrous setting, it was being sung on tape in the hospital room of my very sick husband.

The recovery process was extremely difficult, and definitely not smooth sailing. One night I received a telephone call to come to the hospital right away, because Kibi had developed a high fever, was septic, and dangerously ill. I was really distracted while driving, and in my emotional state I probably shouldn't have been behind the wheel. I made a left turn and was almost T-boned by a car going straight.

I arrived to find an extremely ill husband, with a raging fever so high that his gown was soaked through. I asked about the source of the fever, and was told that they couldn't find the source. I glimpsed above the top of his hospital gown and saw a faint red streak. I pulled the gown down and saw that it was all around his indwelling catheter. I pulled rank and told them to pull out the catheter, culture the tip, and start antibiotics. I was correct—the catheter was indeed the source of the infection, and he improved with treatment.

If all of this wasn't enough, my mother (known as Booba) had a heart attack, and after hospitalization went to a rehabilitation facility and died. My son had two people he adored in his life, his father and his grandmother; he had now lost one, and the other was dangerously ill. He screamed out to me, "Mom, why didn't you let Booba come home? You could have taken care of her and she wouldn't have died."

I replied, "How could I have done that?" I had been taking care of my very sick husband in the hospital, going back and forth to see him, still taking care of the house and the meals, and trying not to completely break down. Well, if I had expected life to be fair, it wasn't.

My mother was buried in June 1995, and my husband said,

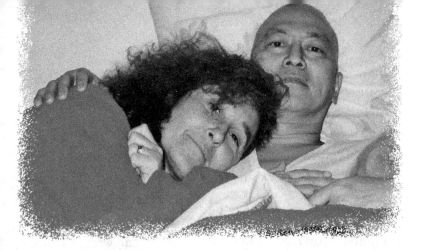

"Deborah tell her I'm too sick to go to the funeral, but I'll be seeing her soon" He'll be seeing her soon? Was this a premonition? I couldn't take much more. I wanted to crawl into a hole and die.

Finally a very weakened Kibi came home from the hospital. Tests showed that the stem cell transplant had not worked, so he was sent for radiation, but that too failed. What devastation. He had been told initially that he had a 70 percent chance of a cure, and here we were after he had endured chemotherapy, a stem cell transplant and radiation, and nothing had worked. He was living a nightmare, and I was, right there living it with him. In my prayers, I swore that I would give ten years of my life if he would be allowed to survive.

He was at home, mainly in bed, and my son helped with his needs while I worked, but the vast majority of his care was on my shoulders. When I asked if I could have someone to help with bathing him, he said, "No, Deborah, I want you to do it," and so I did.

The soundtrack from Schindler's List was on as I walked into the house, the movie about the Holocaust. I asked Kibi why that music was playing, and he said it was because he related to the people who had been in the Holocaust, because only they had approached the terror he was feeling. I am Jewish, my people come from Poland

and Russia, and our family lost many people in the Holocaust. Memories of those abominable times washed over me.

Kibi became weaker and weaker, could hardly eat, and needed oxygen because his lungs were infiltrated by the lymphoma. He also needed pain medication, but was loathe to take any because he was afraid he would be "out of it." I applied the pain patches to his back so he couldn't see them, and increased the dose as needed. Kibi would be on the sofa in the living room, and we had a 50-foot plastic tube connecting him to an oxygen tank in the other room. He would ask, "Deborah, how many litres of oxygen am I on?" and I would answer five. He would then ask me to try to lower it to three, because he didn't want to feel he was sick enough to need five litres.

A delicate dance would then take place. He would ask me to lower the oxygen; I would go into the other room and not lower it, because he needed the maximum amount to breathe; and then he would say, "Did you lower it?" and I would say yes, to three. He would beam, and how wonderful it was to see that flash of my old Kibi, the one before NHL took his smile away. Oh, how I longed to erase the nightmare that our life had become, and return to the wonderful "before NHL" one.

As I mentioned previously, we belonged to a support group, and one of the people we had met was a devout Buddhist. Kibi was Buddhist also, but they belonged to different sects. She once called to ask how he was. I said he was not doing well, and she then began to insist that the reason he wasn't doing well was because he was praying to the wrong sect.

If she had been in the room, I am sure I would have knocked her out with a punch to her jaw. Maybe not, maybe I am exaggerating, but you must feel where I was coming from. You call to support someone, and then tell them basically that it's their own fault they are not doing well; that is unforgivable. What also got to me were people who always talked about being positive, and that if you were not positive, that's why you didn't improve. That is another myth. You are actually not getting better because your illness is very serious, not because you were not exuding positivity.

THE END IS NEAR

Kibi became more and more short of breath, until one day he said, "Deborah, I need to go to the hospital, I can't breathe." He wanted to be sure he was taken to his hospital, and that was achieved. He was in bed on a ward where he as a doctor had treated many patients, and here he now was, a patient himself.

He made me promise not to put him on a respirator, because he said his lungs were shot and he didn't want to be kept alive like that. He also asked for a morphine drip so his breathing could be eased, and he titrated it upwards because of his severe pulmonary problem.

He had been the doctor to many of the other doctors and nurses at the hospital, so when they heard that he was in the hospital, they came to visit him. Many left crying because they said that even though he was so ill himself, he had enquired about their families and themselves.

I basically stayed there around the clock, feeling I was also slipping away but that I needed to be strong for him. What kept me going, I will never know. Before he slipped into a coma he said, "Deb, when I die, I don't want you to remarry." I asked him why, and he said, "Because it would make me jealous." Then don't die. I kept on repeating that over and over in my head like a mantra, trying to make it act as a talisman against the inevitable.

My daughter Rebecca was studying at Pepperdine and going through finals that week, so she could not be in the hospital that day. That turned out to be the final day. My son Keith and I were by his bedside, and his breathing became more erratic. I kept on listening for the next breath, and realized that he was struggling. I said, "Kibi, you can go, you have suffered enough. I will be fine." Oh how I lied, but I could not bear to see him gasp for air when it was hopeless. After I said that to him, he took a breath different from the rest, like saying "thank you," and then the room fell silent. He was gone.

Oh no, it can't be, I thought. *He can't be gone. I want to go too. Don't leave me alone like this. I can't live without you.*

He was pronounced deceased by a good friend of his, a doctor who was on duty in the hospital at the moment, and who had told me that he had been afraid it would be his job to be called to do that. I went home to a house that looked like a florist's store; flowers blanketed the room, their aromas filling up the space. I love flowers, but the cloying smell made me feel sick. I didn't want flowers, I wanted Kibi back. Take back your flowers, give me back my Kibi. No more love, no more wonderful smiles, hugs and fun. It was the end of my world as I knew it.

I decided to bury Kibi in a Buddhist ceremony, to respect his family. My sister Jessica helped me make the arrangements. Another friend picked out a few funeral outfits for me to try on, and after I had chosen one she returned the others to the store. Gestures like that helped more than they could ever know.

Many years before, Kibi had purchased a funeral suit, saying, "Deb, if I need to attend a funeral, I have this one to wear." Little did he know he would be buried in that suit, at his own funeral. I also buried him with his new Varilux spectacles; after all, he couldn't see anything without his glasses, and he would surely need them wherever he was going.

Three hundred people came to the funeral, and each one placed a carnation on his coffin. It was very moving. After the funeral they all came back to my house to eat and reminisce. I was in a trance of disbelief. Was this really happening? Was it possible that I could wake up and realize this was just a bad dream?

Kibi was cremated, and his ashes placed in the Ishida family plot. Rest well, my darling. You were a great person.

LIFE
AFTER
DEATH

I went back to work at CSUN, navigating the 405 freeway back and forth five days a week. How I did it I will never know. My world had been turned upside down, and then it got even worse. My daughter Rebecca said she had to leave because our house felt unstable, like a three-legged table, her dad being the now missing fourth leg. I begged her not to go—it was too soon—but she went anyway; she found an apartment in Brentwood, and just like that she left our house with just two people remaining, my son and myself.

Then Keith chimed in. "Mom, I want to go live with my cousin Karen in Kauai. I don't want to stay here." I tried to tell him I would be all alone, but he went, and I was left rattling around alone in a house that had just recently housed four people, now occupied by one lost and lonely soul. If I had possessed a cyanide capsule, I think I would have taken it, I was so devastated.

Neighbors would ask, "How are you doing?" and then dash past, not even waiting for my response. I wanted to say, "How am I? Can't you see I am sawn in half, and you're asking me how I am?" but they apparently were too embarrassed by it all, not knowing what to say or afraid that widowhood was contagious.

I joined a local grief group for widows, and all seven of us bonded. When we started the group we were all devastated, and kept on saying that if there was a light at the end of the tunnel, none of us could see it. We shared our stories. Some of us had been widowed in a very sudden way, like a car accident, ruptured aneurysm or heart attack, and others had watched our spouses wither away with prolonged illnesses. It was debated as to whether having a sudden death with no chance to say goodbye was better than having a prolonged illness with lots of time to communicate. In the end it was painfully obvious that neither was "better" than the other. We were all grieving widows who would have given ten years of our lives to have our spouses back.

At one session, about a year after the group had formed, the facilitator asked us if any of us had considered dating or having sex again. Everyone decided that I would lead the way, but they were wrong; quite a few of them dated before I did, and later on a couple of them remarried.

At one session we were discussing something, and we all burst into raucous laughter. "Ha ha ha, oh my goodness, my belly hurts." We were so loud that a counselor next door who was leading a group knocked on the door and asked us to please keep the noise down. He also asked, "What kind of group is this?" to which we replied in peals of laughter, "We are the widows group!"

Could it be possible that the group of us who had been so devastated were now able to laugh out loud? It didn't mean that we had "gotten over" the deaths of our husbands, but we had been able to let a little bit of light penetrate the pitch-black darkness.

As time went on, my son Keith came home from Hawaii for a while, and my daughter Rebecca got married. Keith stepped in for his father and we both walked her down the aisle. So life went on, but my beloved Kibi wasn't there, making life so very different than it would have been otherwise. The sun still rose in the east and set in the west, there were still twenty-four hours in a day, but my days were veiled in sadness.

Kibi's full name, Kibimaro, means "shining," so I called him "sunshine boy," and that fit him to a T; he spread sunshine wherever he went. He was a phenomenal husband, father, brother, physician, uncle and friend. He has missed out on walking his daughter Rebecca down the aisle, but was spared her divorce, and he has not had the pleasure of seeing his two wonderful grandchildren—Emily, who is currently 16, and Ethan, 19. I will love him forever, and Kibi, I want you to know that I am so happy that you chose me, and "I miss you like crazy."

So the question is, can I carry on? Can life have any meaning for me? Or did it disappear for me when Kibi died? I can tell you that this is not what I would have chosen; my dream was to grow old with him, not lose him at the age of 51. We had talked about dividing the year into three parts: four months each year in Hawaii, four months on his family land in Calistoga, and four months in Los Angeles. But as the old Yiddish saying goes, "Man makes plans, and God laughs."

However, I have carried on, and have had some wonderful life experiences. I did start to date, and have had four long-term relationships in the 25 years since I lost my beloved spouse. I think I heeded Kibi's last words that he didn't want me to marry, because all the men I dated were not marriage material.

Keith, my son, has been home from Hawaii for four years and lives with me. He gardens, and I have learned to prepare beets 20 ways!! Keith is now almost the same age as when Kibi died, and he resembles his father so much. He drives very cautiously, like his father did; I am more of a speed demon. Being in the car with him takes me back in time when Kibi and I would be in the car together. I would tell Kibi to go faster, and he would say, "Deborah there's a stop sign ahead." I would say, "Yes, a mile ahead!" I also love my daughter Rebecca and my grandchildren Emily and Ethan, and it's a joy to see the grandkids grow into wonderful human beings.

I have also pursued my acting dreams that I had as a child, but never really accomplished because of medicine, marriage and motherhood. I am in SAG-AFTRA (a labor union for actors), have done a couple of commercials, been on TV, and have appeared in plays and short films. I am by no means a well-known actress, but I have had a modicum of success.

My biggest love is stand-up comedy, and I have pursued it now for several years. I have even performed many times at the famous Comedy Store on Sunset Boulevard. During the COVID pandemic I have done virtual stand-up on Zoom, and while I miss the roar of the audience, I still love it. So here I am in the twilight of my life, wondering what I will do when I grow up, which to me proves that I have a lot of life still left in me

To all of my fellow people who grieve out there, I say I love you, hold on tight, you may feel devastated now, but there definitely is light at the end of the tunnel, and I send you all a giant hug.

THE END

WHAT IS THIS THING CALLED GRIEF?

There are several definitions. Grief is a deep sorrow, especially that comes by someone's death. Grief is a normal process of responding to a loss. These definitions, however, cannot possibly embody what it means to have lost someone dear to you.

I am a widow, so for me I grieve for the loss of my spouse. Others grieve for the loss of a significant other, a parent, a sibling, a child. Whomever we have lost, for them we grieve.

Death comes like a thief in the night, stealing our loved ones away from us. We are then expected to "get over it." We are expected to carry on as if nothing happened, or if it did, that it was minor. We are definitely not to make anyone feel uncomfortable. We are expected to accept that old friends will disappear without a trace. We got casseroles when our loved ones died, but now we do not get asked out to lunch, dinner, or even to coffee. We have to fill up the gas tank in our car, and do all the finances. We have to change names on mortgages, bank accounts and credit cards. When we cross their names off of an account we feel as if we have eliminated them from our lives, and we feel guilty.

The world looks bizarre. You might as well be on Venus. You sob when you see couples holding hands. You sit alone at the dining table, but still set a place for him that he will never use.

You push through the day, and those with young children need to take care of their wants. Unless you have a lot of money, you need to go to work. You want to be with him now, and sometimes think you would be better off dead. You keep his old shirt, and sleep in it so you can smell his scent.

If your spouse died of suicide or an overdose, there is even more guilt involved. You debate if it is better that your husband died suddenly, or that he had a prolonged illness so you would have been able to say goodbye.

Although we all grieve, we do it differently, and our timetables are not the same.

People ask, "How long does grief last?" They want to get out of it, but then feel that by doing so they are betraying the memory of their spouse. Most people begin to see some lifting of grief at about the one-year mark, but some grieve for years. Don't be ashamed to seek counselling if your grief is prolonged, or you feel like harming yourself.

There are five stages of grief described by Elisabeth Kubler-Ross:

Denial,

Anger,

Bargaining,
Depression and
Acceptance.

There is also complicated grief—physical, psychological or emotional abuse that never healed.

Thank you for reading my book. This is my journey through love and loss, and while yours is unique, we are all fellow travelers here. Breathe, take the day one second at a time, put one foot in front of the other, and be good to yourself. Remember, "this too shall pass."

BIOGRAPHY

Deborah Ishida was born in England and moved to the US after college. She attended medical school at UCLA, then worked for many years as a Family Practice M.D. She married the love of her life, had two children, and had a very happy life until her husband was prematurely taken from her as a result of Non-Hodgkin's Lymphoma at the age of 51. After a long period of grieving, Ishida began the next phase of her life, pursuing acting, stand-up comedy, reading to children and teaching for the National Alliance on Mental Illness. She is the proud grandmother of two wonderful grandchildren who unfortunately never met their grandfather. She is proof that there is light at the end of the tunnel, and would like everyone to know that that light is there for all who grieve the loss of a loved one.

9 781662 921056